FIRE YOUR ACCOUNTANT

BASIC BUSINESS ACCOUNTING IN 7 DAYS

By

Senthilmani Mayooran ACMA CGMA, MSc, BSc.
&
Senthilmani Thuvarakan MSc, CIMA Passed Finalist.

MAYOORAN & THUVARAKAN

Copyright © 2013 Senthilmani Mayooran & Senthilmani Thuvarakan

All rights reserved.

ISBN: 978-1494464103
ISBN-10: 1494464101

DEDICATION

We would like to thank our parents for guiding and mentoring us throughout our childhood to become experts in our professional life, and this book is dedicated to them.

CONTENTS

ACKNOWLEDGEMENTS

CHAPTER 1:   1
GETTING STARTED

CHAPTER 2:   15
MONEY MATTERS

CHAPTER 3:   25
CONTROL YOUR COST

CHAPTER 4:   33
THE BASIC TAX FOR YOUR BUSINESS

CHAPTER 5:   39
HOW TO ANALYSE YOUR PERFORMANCE

CHAPTER 6:   49
EMPLOYING STAFF FOR THE FIRST TIME

CHAPTER 7:   53
BENEFITS OF VIRTUAL BOOKKEEPING WITH CLOUD CFO IN THE DIGITAL AGE

ACKNOWLEDGMENTS

We would like to express our gratitude to the many people who gave us assistance through this book; to all those who provided support, offered feedback, and assisted in the editing, proofreading and design.

We would like to thank DVG STAR LTD in guiding us to publish this book. Without their guidance and support we could not even think about publishing this book.

We would like to thank Dayna Plummer for helping us in the process of editing.

Last but not least, we would like to thank our parents and teachers for guiding and mentoring us throughout our childhood to become experts in our professional life, and the success of the book is dedicated to them.

GETTING STARTED

MAYOORAN & THUVARAKAN

CHAPTER 1

What is accounting?

Accounting is the systematic process of recording, reporting and analysing the financial transactions of a business. In simple terms accounting helps a firm to identify whether the business is profitable or not.

The accountant who is responsible for maintaining the accounts of the company is expected to follow accounting principles and standards such as generally accepted accounting practices, also known as GAAP.

Which accounting is for you?

There are several types of accounting practiced in the corporate world, including financial accounting, management accounting, governmental accounting, tax accounting, forensic accounting, project accounting, and social accounting.

As a SME owner you should give priority to financial accounting and management accounting.

Financial accounting: The process of producing financial statements for external use. The financial statements will include the past and present performance of the business following certain accounting standards known as GAAP. There are many accounting systems available to prepare financial accounting, for example: sage line 50, QuickBooks and SAP.

Management accounting: Prepared for the internal use of the company. This takes place in the form of budgeting, cost accounting and so on. This is where management needs to place higher priority as this will highlight the key performance indicators of the company, for example: sales, labour cost and food cost.

Accounting: how it works

The concept of accounting starts with the ideology of double entry. In simple terms, double entry means each and every transaction has a debit and credit effect. Given that the revenue is equal to the expenses of the company we can arrive at the fundamental formula of double entry,

Assets = liabilities + equity

For example if we take cash sales, the double entry for this will be as follows,

Cash – debit

Sales – credit

As the cash is coming in to the business it is debited and the sales are credited. We follow a standard practice for double entry which will clearly communicate which entry should be debited and credited.

	Debit	Credit
Asset	Increase	Decrease
Liability	Decrease	Increase
Income	Decrease	Increase
Expense	Increase	Decrease
Shareholders' Equity	Decrease	Increase

The table above provides a clear picture about the basic double entry techniques used in accounting.

Now let's look at some of the basic definitions of accounting terms used in accounting practices:

Asset – Any item of economic value owned by the company. For example: land, furniture, property, and so on. Assets can be mainly classified as long term assets, current assets (short term), and intangible assets (goodwill of the business).

Liability – Liability is an obligation a company needs to pay. It can be in the form of debt or suppliers payments. Liabilities can be classified as current liabilities, which are the debt which needs to be settled within one year, and long term liabilities which are the debt which needs to be settled over a longer period (more than one year).

Income – The total amount of money generated by the company for goods sold and services provided during a certain time period.

Expenses – Any cost of running the business.

Shareholders' equity – An ownership stake in the company in the form of common stocks or preferred stock. It can also be calculated by deducting total liabilities from the total assets of the company.

Financial statement: what does it include?

Income statement – Accounting of revenue, expenses, and net profit for a certain period. The period can be on a quarterly or yearly basis. The income statement is based on the fundamental equation,

Income = Revenue – Expenses

Income statements will help you to identify whether the profits margin the business is generating is in line with industry standards.

Balance sheet – Indicates the financial condition of a company at a specific time period. The first part of the balance sheet includes the assets a company owns and the second part includes the source of financing.

Cash flow statements – Enable the management and investors to understand where cash is coming from and where the cash has been spent.

Which business structure is for you?

When you are structuring your business it is very important to select the correct business structure, as it is going to affect the amount of tax you are going to pay and the paper work you have to do.

The most common forms of business are:

- Sole proprietorship
- Partnership
- Corporation
- Limited liability Company (LLC)

Sole Proprietorship

If you intend to work on your own, this structure will best suit your needs. Under sole proprietorship the owner is responsible for the debt. The business structure is very simple and easy to set up.

The external source of financing will be very difficult for sole proprietorship. In these instances the owner has to rely on his savings or investments.

Partnership

If you intend to operate with several business partners, then a partnership is the structure you must choose. A partnership can be classified by two types:

- General partnership
- Limited partnership

General partnership is where several partners manage the business and take responsibility for the business obligations.

Limited partnership involves both the general and limited partners. The general partner's role will be similar to the general partnership. On the other hand, limited partners serve as investors only. They will not have any ownership stake in the company.

The main benefit of a limited partnership is tax savings; you don't need to pay tax on your income. You can pass it on to the profit or loss you made during the period.

On the negative side, general partners are responsible for business obligations. In addition, it is more expensive to set up than sole proprietorship, as it requires more legal and accounting services.

Corporation

A corporation is an independent legal entity, and it is very complex and difficult to set up. However the benefit which arises from this model is you are not responsible for the business obligations, so your personal assets are not at risk.

Another plus is the availability of financing: the corporation can issue stocks to raise funds. It can be in the form common stocks or preferred stocks.

The downside of a corporation is the cost involved with preparing accounting and tax returns. As the business structure is more complex you need the advice from an attorney as well.

Another drawback of a corporation structure is you may need to pay double tax. The corporation should pay the corporation tax applicable to them. The second form of tax comes with dividends. One possible way to overcome this double taxation is to increase the compensation for the partners. But it is very important to study the maximum compensation allowed in accounting standards for business partners.

Limited Liability Company

A Limited Liability Company (LLC) is a hybrid company which brings in the features of both a partnership and a corporation. The partners are not responsible for the business obligations, and it avoids the double taxation.

An LLC doesn't have any limitations on the number of shareholders a company can have. Furthermore, the shareholders can be involved in the business practices.

You should always keep in mind that when you are using a LLC structure you should use an experienced accountant who has a sound knowledge in several accounting practices.

Government bodies, registering and filing

Registering your business with companies house

When you are planning to register your business you must have the following information with you:

Company Name and Address – It is a rule of thumb that you cannot use an existing business name. You can always check the availability of the name in the company registration web portal. If the name already exists you have to find an alternative name for your business.

Officer Details (Director and Secretary) – To set up a private limited company you should have at least one director who is over 16 years old. You can also have a secretary for your entity but it is not mandatory. You should have the following information before registering the name of directors and secretaries:

- **Full name**

- **Residential address** - This can be the registered address. The address should also mention the state or country where the address is situated.

- **Nationality, occupation, date of birth and any former names** (that have been used for business purposes in the last 20 years).

- **'Consent to act' information** – In order to meet the signature requirement you may need to provide any 3 of the following:

    - Last three digits of your telephone number

    - Last three digits of your National Insurance number

    - Last three digits of your Passport number

    - Your Mother's maiden name

    - Your Eye Colour

    - Father's first name

Share Capital and Shareholder Details – You must submit the name and address of the shareholders of your entity. Furthermore you should also mention the amount of shareholdings owned by the shareholders.

Payment – You can make payment via debit card or credit card after setting up an online account.

Starting a company or organisation and Corporation Tax with regulations

When you are registering your entity it is very important to communicate the existence of your entity to revenue and customs for tax purposes and other legal matters. This guide explains what you need to do and when.

New companies and organisations and Corporation Tax

When you set up a new company or organisation that's liable for Corporation Tax you must:

- You must communicate your business existence within a certain time period, for example, within 3 months.
- You must pay your tax obligations on time
- You must file your tax return on time

When you are registering your company with revenue and customs, they will use the information you have provided to set up a computer record for your entity. Then they will create a unique reference number, known as a UTR (unique tax payer reference number).

They then send a form called Corporation Tax Information for New Companies to your company's registered office. The form will also include your UTR, so please keep that reference number in a safe place. You need it when you are contacting revenue and customs in relation to a tax query.

Using revenue and customs online services

If you used the revenue and customs online service your company will be automatically enrolled for corporate taxation online and then revenue and customs will post you the pin within seven days.

It is very important that you keep that pin very safe. You should validate the pin within short time span.

Using an accountant or tax adviser to deal with revenue and customs

You can appoint an accountant or tax adviser - known to revenue and customs as an agent - to deal with revenue and customs on your behalf. The agent will communicate the tax position of your company on your behalf.

Record keeping for Corporation Tax

If your company or organisation is liable for Corporation Tax, you must keep and retain adequate business and accounting records to file an accurate Company Tax Return and calculate how much Corporation Tax you need to pay. If you need more help and to claim your gift please visit www.YourCloudCFO.com

MONEY MATTERS

CHAPTER 2

Every new business needs money during the starting-up process. This is to buy equipment, establish the office, to pay the bills, for marketing and so on. This all before the first sale is made.

You have to choose the right financing option in the first place, and to do so you have to evaluate the advantages and disadvantages of the available financing options. This book will help you to analyse and choose the best options available to you according to your specific needs and circumstances.

In order to work out your financial requirements, you have to prepare a business plan. This business plan should include information about your business operation and essential financial forecasts. A good business plan will help you to convince your bank or other potential sources of finance that you know what you are doing and their money will be safe with less risk.

You must have accurate idea of your financial requirements, as your customers may not pay you immediately. It's better to prepare a weekly cash flow forecast for the next 6 months.

Financing Options available to you during the start-up period

1. **Use your own money**
   You can consider doing a re-mortgage, or using a credit card or unsecured personal loan, or selling assets, etc.

   Advantages

   - You will have more control, as there is no need to give any return or any shares to others
   - No need to worry about outside investors withdrawing their support at any time

   Disadvantages

   - Possibilities of losing your home or assets in case your business fails
   - Puts pressure on you and your family

2. **Family and friends**
   You have to consider the worst case scenario of losing their money if your business fails.

   Advantages

   - May offer easy terms, such as interest free

Disadvantages

- Pressure on you and your relationship with them

3. Borrow from banks by creating a credible business plan

Advantage

- You can match the term of a loan to your requirements
- Less family pressure

Disadvantage

- The need to do a regular payment might cause cash flow problems
- You may have to offer some security

4. Outside investors to finance your business

You could issue ordinary shares to investors in return for their capital

Advantages

- Bring additional expertise and funding
- No need to pay until you can afford to pay

Disadvantages

- You may have to share your business and profits
- Investors may want control over how you manage the business

Possible sources of finance available to you after the start-up period

Retained profits: This is the net earnings which arise after you pay the tax. During the initial stage of the company's life cycle it is rare you will be paying dividends. The company only focuses on business expansion and rapid growth. These retained earnings can be kept for future investment. It is a very useful technique to fund business expansion.

Bank overdraft: Bank overdraft will be provided by the bank, and it depends on your credit rating. If you are a start-up, the amount you can borrow will be limited. Overdraft is a very useful technique for short term cash flow issues, such as making payments to suppliers. It should be noted that it comes with an interest cost.

Trade Credit: This approach is a very useful technique. Trade credit means you are delaying the payment to your suppliers. Once again it depends heavily on your bargaining power. If your bargaining power is high then you can demand a higher credit period. On the other hand if your bargaining power is low you may need to make a payment immediately. To use this technique in an effective and efficient way you have to build relationships and enhance the trust between you and suppliers.

Hire purchase: This approach is where you make an initial down payment and make the rest of the payment as equal instalments. You have to bear the interest cost. At the end of the hire purchase period the assets belongs to you.

Leasing: This approach is similar to the hire purchase. The only difference is at the end of the leasing period the asset doesn't belong to you. This technique can be used when you don't want to own the assets.

Long term Bank loan: Borrowing options from the bank can be a fixed interest loan or variable interest loan. When you are borrowing you should make sure whether your business is generating sufficient cash flow to make loan repayments. You need to provide collateral to borrow the money.

Issue of additional share: Shares can be issued to attract more capital to the business. The issue with this approach is the ownership of your business will be diluted and the new investors might have a different view about the business.

Why use a business bank account?

When you register the company, next important step to follow is open a separate business bank account. This is to distinguish your personal bank account from your business bank account. The cash inflow and outflow should be carried out using the business bank account.

This systematic approach not only will allow you to have an accurate tracking system but will also be very useful during tax filling and audit periods.

When you are opening your business account please check for the following features

- company debit card
- company credit card
- overdraft and loan facilities
- asset finance
- commercial mortgage

Collecting money from your customers

If you are a service provider or selling goods to your customers you need to invoice the customers. If you are registered for Value Added Tax (VAT) then you can claim VAT in your invoice. If not, you cannot claim the VAT. If you need advice on registering for VAT please visit www.YourCloudCFO.com.

As a business you might have one-off customers and long term customers. With one-off customers you don't need to build the relationship, as you will collect your payments immediately. The issues come with a long term customer who has the potential to buy your services or goods on a continuous basis.

The customers will ask for extended credit periods. You may be forced to agree with their credit terms if your business depends heavily on their buying power. The delay in their payments can create cash flow issues to you.

Here are some things to remember when calling past-due customers:

Understand the negotiation process – Negotiation involves the skills you have develop as the business owner. If you have a better understanding with each other, then there won't be any issues in your relationship.

Focus on a win-win solution – Create a win - win solution for both parties. Listen to your customers and understand their cash flow problems, but you should also put a credit limit on each customer. This can be made based on their earnings potential.

Be patient and confident – Most of the time the common mistake all of us make is to demand for an immediate payment. It can ruin the entire relationship you have built. So it is also important to develop your patience skills and to be confident about your customers.

CONTROL YOUR COST

CHAPTER 3

Keeping track of business cost

Keeping track of your business cost is very important. If you don't have a proper tracking method you may have a wrong picture about your business model. At the end it is all about the net cash flow your business is generating.

Business incurs several costs including production cost, labour cost, administrative cost, distribution cost and so on. When you record all these costs it will give a clear picture of where your money is going out.

You can use accounting software or systems such as sage accounts or QuickBooks to record your income and expenses.

When evaluating the business, performance management accounting comes into play. You can prepare the basic management accounting in an excel sheet. Forget about the model, just enter the cash inflow and cash outflow your business incurs during the year on a regular basis.

Then do a variance analysis using the previous year's data. For larger variances conduct an investigation. Find out solutions to reduce the cost.

For example last year your labour cost was £60,000 and this year it has increased to £80,000. The variance is £20,000. There can be several reasons for that increase. It may be due to additional shifts. To find out whether the additional shifts have increased your revenue will give a clear picture about that cost.

Cash is the king

A business cannot survive without cash inflow in the long run. This is where you should always prepare cash flow statements. This approach identifies whether your business is generating sufficient cash to manage your expenses.

The cash conversion cycle is also key in running a business. The cash conversion cycle can be calculated as follows:

CCC = receivable days + payable days – inventory days

Sample Cash Flow Forecast

Week Ending	05/01/2014	12/01/2014	19/01/2014	26/01/2014
Opening Balance	100,000	91,000	96,500	103,000
Bank- TO CREDIT				
Expected Sales	12,000	10,000	14,000	10,000
Net cash inflow	112,000	101,000	110,500	113,000
Unpresented Chq	1,500			
Direct debits	1,000	2,000	1,000	500
Rent	5,000			
Business Rates	1,000			
Wages	5,000			
Loan Repayments	5,000			
Corporations Tax				1,000
PAYE			4,000	
VAT				10,000
Cheque run	2,500	2,500	2,500	2,500
Total Expenses	21,000	4,500	7,500	14,000
Expected Closing Bank Balance	91,000	96,500	103,000	99,000

You should also prepare cash flow projections, which you can prepare in an excel sheet. Project the sales income as per the last year, then identify the cost which will be debited from your bank account. This can includes direct debit such as electricity, rents, business rates, and supplier payments.

This approach will enable you to manage cash flow issues. Planning in advance always helps for a rainy day.

Budgeting

Budgeting is where you prepare your financial projections for next year using this year's data. Using budgeting, you can set targets for your departments or branches. Setting performance related tasks are always a confident boost for store managers and staff.

Sample Forecasted budget

FORECASTED SALES 2014-15	520,000
Cost of Sales	156,000
Cost of Sales %	30.00%
Labour	130,000
Labour %	**25.00%**
Total Direct Cost	286,000
Gross profit	234,000
Gross profit Margin %	45.00%
Expenses	
Rent	40,000
Service charges	5,000
Water	2,000
Rates	2,000
Insurance	1,000
Electricity	10,000
Security charges	8,000
Postage & stationery	2,000
Telephone	4,000
Advertising	2,500
IT	3,000
Repairs & maintanance	10,000
Cleaning	10,000
Clothing	1,000
Total Expenses	100,500
Operating profit	**133,500**
Operating profit %	**25.67%**

THE BASIC TAX FOR YOUR BUSINESS

CHAPTER 4

What is VAT?

VAT is a tax charged when a VAT registered company is selling products and services to their customers. On the other hand the VAT registered company can claim VAT for the products and services they have paid.

There are three rates of VAT:

- standard
- reduced
- zero

There are also some goods and services that are exempt from VAT.

In order to register yourself for VAT purposes, you have to be in a business which is generating income on a continuous basis. One-off income will not qualify you for VAT registration purposes.

When you must register for VAT

If you're in a business which is selling products and services which can be taxed, then you should register yourself with Revenues & Customs for claiming VAT.

For example, in the UK you can register yourself with Revenues & Customs if you meet the following criteria:

- Your Business turnover exceeded £79,000 last year.
- You estimate that the turnover will exceed the £79,000 limit very soon.

How VAT is charged and accounted for

The VAT you claim from your selling of goods and services is called output tax, and the VAT you pay on the purchase of goods and services is called input tax.

Filling in your VAT Return

If you are registered for VAT then you must file your VAT return on a timely basis, generally known as quarterly basis. The VAT return should include the output tax, input tax and the net tax.

If the output tax is higher than the input tax, you have to make the net payment to Revenues & Customs. This can be a direct debit or BACS payment. On the other hand if the input tax is higher than the output tax, you can claim the net from the Revenues & Customs.

Exempt items

There are few items which are not covered by VAT. A few examples are:

- Insurance
- Providing credit
- Education and training, if certain conditions are met
- Charity fundraising
- Services provided by doctors and nurses.

Corporate Tax

What is Corporation Tax?

Corporation tax is a tax charged on the net taxable income of companies.

Taxable profits for Corporation Tax include:

- Trading profit
- Capital gains
- Investment profit, not the dividend

What is an accounting period for Corporation Tax?

Generally it is considered to be a 12 month period. It is very important to note that you cannot choose your tax period.

Do you need Tax Adviser?

You can directly deal with Revenues & Customs in relation to tax purposes, or you can assign a tax adviser. You can save a lot of money by implementing tax planning and using good tax advice. A **virtual tax adviser** will be a great value addition for your business with a very affordable cost.

If you need more advice on filing your company tax return and paying tax, please contact your local Revenues & Customs. They will be happy to help you.

HOW TO ANALYSE YOUR PERFORMANCE

CHAPTER 5

How to use ratios analysis to identify financial performance

Ratio analysis is a key tool in analysing the financial statements of a company. As financial statements represent past and present data, it can be a very complex for a reader to understand. With the use of ratio analysis, a reader or investor will be able to understand the financial performance of a company.

Below are some of the key financial ratios which can be used for financial analysis of a company.

Profitability ratios

Profitability measures can be used to measure the ability of the company to generate profitability. The profitability ratios can be compared with the historical figures or with peer companies to identify its current position. Under this we are going to discuss two profit margins: gross profit margin and net profit margin.

Gross profit margin

You can calculate the gross profit margin as follows:

Gross profit margin = gross profit/ net sales

Gross profit can be calculated by deducting the cost of sales from net sales. Generally the cost of sales includes raw material cost, labour cost and manufacturing cost.

This ratio measures the ability of the management to efficiently reduce the cost of sales. A higher ratio is considered to be a more favourable one for the business.

Net profit margin

You can calculate the net profit margin as follows:

Net profit margin = net income/ net sales

This is the bottom line profit. Net income can be calculated by adding other incomes from gross profit and by subtracting other expenses from the total gross income.

This formula measures the ability of management to control administrative expenses, distribution expenses and other expenses.

For example – a company is making a sufficient gross profit margin but the net profit margin is negative. The reason for this a higher finance cost.

By comparing both the gross profit margin and net profit margin we can arrive at a better conclusion.

Return on capital employed

You can calculate the ROCE as follows:

ROCE = Earnings before interest tax/capital employed

Capital employed = (debt + shareholders equity)/2

This approach measures the ability of the business to generate return on total capital employed.

Shareholders are the people who invested in the business with a certain amount of return for their investment. Additionally as a business owner you will also borrow to fund future expansion or refurbishment. So this ROCE calculates whether the business is generating sufficient return to cover the shareholders' expectations and interest expenses.

Gearing ratio

You can calculate the gearing ratio as follows:

Gearing = total liabilities/shareholders' equity

This ratio measures the leverage position of the company. Generally 50% - 60% gearing level is an acceptable level. Anything beyond that level can lead to serious consequences, like the company struggling to make the interest payments and the bank taking over your assets.

Current ratio

The current ratio is used to analyse the liquidity of the company. In simple terms it ascertain whether the business' short term assets are sufficient enough to cover its short term obligations. It can be calculated as follows:

Current ratio = current assets/current liabilities

A higher current ratio is not good for the company and vice versa. However, it is very important to understand that this is not only the liquidity measure of the company. Understanding the types of short term assets a company has and how quickly they can be converted into cash will give a better understanding about the company's liquidity position.

How to Identify and implement Your KPI

As the CEO of a business you must set strategic goals for your business. They can vary from business to business. For example: if you are running a business with a motive to make money, then your KPI will be based on profitability measures such as gross profit, pre-tax profit and so on.

On the other hand if you are running a not-for-profit organization your goal will be more focused on achieving non-profit measures such as the number of people who benefited from your organization, your contribution to social developments in the form building schools and so on.

It is very important to understand that KPI should be quantifiable. Once you set the target for your business you can easily implement set ideas to work towards that goal. Each year you can review your performance and can add more value to your shareholders.

Balanced scorecard and its usefulness

Balanced scorecard is a strategic performance management framework that allows management to identify strategic priorities. According to these priorities, the management can design and implement goals and measures to evaluate how well they are executing their strategic goal. The balanced scorecard measures the organization performance in four metrics. They are:

- Financial perspective
- Customer perspective
- Internal perspective
- Learning and growth perspective

You can use a balanced scorecard to improve the organizational performance by aligning performance related pay with it. If the management achieves their target, they will be rewarded with a bonus; if not, they will not be rewarded a bonus and will be subject to investigation.

For example – you are running five burger shops in London, and they are managed by five different management teams. You identify that the performance in 2 shops was excellent the last two years, but currently has started to decline. For the rest of the burger shops the performances are steady but can be improved, as the burger shops are strategically located near schools, hospitals, and office complexes.

When you are investigating the reason for the deteriorating performance of the 2 shops with the management, they replied that the staff working in their shops are not motivated. The reason for this de-motivation is irrespective of their best performance during the last year, they have been treated similarly to the rest of the shops.

Now you have identified that there is a critical need for performance related pay, and it is very important to implement it as soon as possible.

In order to implement this policy, you have identified 5 KPI of your business and planning to set a target for each KPI. The KPIs are sales, food cost, labour cost, customer service and net profit.

For each of these KPIs you have to set target measures which the management needs to achieve. Now let's find out how you can set the BSC.

The performance measures are set for a quarter:

Sales target - £120,000

Food cost – 30% of the sales

Labour cost – 25% of the sales

Customer service – reduce the number of customer complaints to 10.

Net profit – 10% of the sales

Now you should set points ranging from 0 – 1 for each target measure. If the management achieves the target they will be awarded 1 point; if not, 0 points will be awarded. Now the maximum points a store can achieve is 5 and the lowest is 0.

If a management team achieves 5 points they will be eligible for the high performance related pay. Achieving 4 points will enable them to get bonus, but it will be lower than the previous one. Anything below 4 points will not be eligible for a bonus. If the management scores below 1 or 2 they will be subject to investigation and proper actions should be taken to improve performance in future.

These target measures will motivate your team members to achieve the strategic goals. If you don't have a proper goal it can be really de-motivating for top performers in your company. You can always add more insights to these performance measures and can enhance shareholders' wealth.

EMPLOYING STAFF FOR THE FIRST TIME

CHAPTER 6

If you are preparing to hire your first employee, you should approach it with caution. It is very important to hire a suitable candidate to add value to your organization. The selected candidate should be trustworthy. Apart from those issues there are several legal factors which you should take into account when hiring new employees.

Employing Staff for the First Time - In almost every country it is legally very important to meet the minimum wages, so before hiring anyone you should find out the minimum wages in your country. For example, in the UK, the minimum wage is £6.31 per hour for employees over 21 years old as of Oct 2013. If the legal body, which is the HMRC in the UK, finds out that you are not paying the minimum wages they will send you the arrears payment you have to make plus a penalty for not making minimum wages payments.

Check the Legal Status to Work - This is critical when you are hiring foreign workers. Some of them might be students and their work hours will be limited to certain hours. You can research their work rights on the VISA page. If you are unable to find out, you are free to contact legal bodies to find out their working rights.

Obtain Employer's Liability Insurance – you should get your employer's liability insurance coverage as soon as you have registered yourself as an employer. This liability coverage is useful when your employees have injured themselves at work or if they get work-related illness such as stress and so on.

Terms and Conditions of the Employment – you should give written statements of employment contract to your employee. This should clearly communicate the roles and responsibilities of the selected candidate.

Sometimes as an employer you may need to invest a huge amount in training. If the selected candidate leaves after the training process, your loss is severe. In these instances you can specify the penalty payments the employee needs to make before leaving and the period of notice they have to give.

Registering your Business as an Employer – you have to register your business as an employer with the legal entity in your country. For example, in the UK you have to register yourself with the HMRC as an employer. After registering yourself, the HMRC will send you the PAYE reference number and accounts office reference.

BENEFITS OF VIRTUAL BOOKKEEPING AND CLOUD CFO IN THE DIGITAL AGE

CHAPTER 7

What is Virtual Bookkeeping?

Virtual bookkeeping is where a professionally qualified accountant carries out your routine bookkeeping virtually. It can be carried out from a home or any part of the world.

How They Work

The basic requirement for this operation is a high-speed internet connection and access to cloud accounting software.

Once you set up a cloud network for your company, the bookkeeper will access your server to perform the necessary tasks. Alternatively, you can totally outsource your bookkeeping to be managed from their server and perform all the work for you.

Send your financial data
- Bank statements
- Supplier invoices
- Payroll iformation
- Other informations

Accounting Tasks will be performed
- Enter all transactions
- Process payroll
- Bank reconciliation
- VAT return
- Other necessary tasks

Real time Accounting Solutions
- Monthly management accounts
- Cashflow forecasting
- Age creditors report
- And more

Benefits of switching to virtual accountants

Cost reduction – We are all affected by the economic crisis. Every business is under severe pressure to cut costs. A virtual accountant is the gateway to reduce your business costs.

Instead of running a team of 5 accountants, you can choose to hire one accountant and the rest is done with a virtual accountant. The cost saving will be almost by 50% however this is subject to your business models and complexities. Using these savings in cost, you can invest in business developments. This will helps you to grow your business rapidly.

Secondly, a virtual accountant reduces the hardware and upgrade costs.

Thirdly, you can use the office space to implement a sales team or other professional team members who really take part in the end products or services delivered to the customers.

Focus on core competence – if you are an entrepreneur you should focus on your core competence and how you can add more value

to the end products or services. If you focus more on accounting during the initial stages, you may be overtaken by your competitors. So your virtual accountant helps you to focus on key business principles and enhancing the value addition to the customers. You don't need to worry about staff leaving or holiday coverage, etc.

Flexibility – Virtual accounting is very flexible. You can hire virtual accountants based on your requirements: on a weekly basis, monthly basis, or yearly basis.

Anytime anywhere access – As we all are in the information age, the real benefit of virtual accounting is you can access it from your business, home, or any part of the world. This access enables you to make better decisions on time.

Qualified Accountants – You could have a team made up of people of top caliber in the accounting profession, holding professional qualifications such as CIMA, ACCA, ACA, CPA, etc., and exposure to the big four firms is also great value addition to your business model.

Is your confidentially being compromised?

The main question behind a third party virtual accountant is whether confidentiality is being compromised.

It is fair to say that a business' key information can fall in to the wrong party's hands, such as competitors or the media. The consequences may be severe depending on the information which is leaked. You have to make sure each and every staff member is obliged to follow the ethical codes, which is to meet client confidentiality.

A **Service Level Agreement (SLA)** can be developed to protect your confidentiality when you have decided to move along with a third party accountant. The service level agreement can classify the duties and responsibilities of each party. It can also be done with the help of lawyers.

What happens when the server crashes?

By conducting regular backups you will be protected from server crashes. The backups can be done on a weekly basis, and you can create a separate folder to keep your backup files. When the system crashes you can use your backup files.

How to Choose Your Service Level Package

You have to shop around and choose a customised package to meet your requirements. Running a business is not only about bookkeeping; you should be able to identify the key performance indicators in your business, internal control weakness, how to reduce the borrowing cost, and so on.

As an entrepreneur or start-up you will be facing cash flow issues in hiring a Chief Financial Officer (CFO). In order to fill this gap you can negotiate and ask for your Cloud CFO, who will be assisting you and will be providing you with the necessary financial advisory services.

Benefits of Having Your Cloud CFO with Virtual Bookkeeping Services

- Hiring a CFO to assist you is expensive. Having access to Free CFO advice when required will be enough during the start-up period until you grow bigger.

- You will have a good reporting structure which highlights your business performance.

- It is not about just bookkeeping. Monthly performance reviews can be very useful to boost your business.

- Monthly management accounting – this can clearly highlight your profit margin, labour and food cost as a percentage of sales, and so on.

- Control weaknesses and risk assessment – it is very important to place tight internal controls and external systems in place. Without these systems, even if you make sufficient money you cannot run your business in the long run. The CFO will recommend to you the possible systems you can implement to control your weaknesses.

- Cash flow forecasting – the main purpose of running a business is to enhance shareholders' wealth. In order to do so you should always plan your income and expenses in advance. This will help you to control unnecessary borrowings, cheques bouncing, or poor relationships with suppliers due to not releasing payments on time.

- Investment appraisal – as you grow you may need to buy new business ventures. You can ask your Cloud CFO to assist you in valuing the business using several techniques, such as free cash flow, EV multiples and so on. This valuation will stop you from paying too much for a buyout.

- The CFO will also highlight for you the potential synergies available to you via mergers and acquisitions.

- Unbiased decision making – decision making is one of the keys to the success of a business, and should be made on time. An in-house CFO might make decisions to maximise his own wealth. But with the use of your Cloud

CFO, this biased decision making is eliminated. Your Cloud CFO will recommend to you the most suitable cause of action plans for your business needs.

To claim your free gift please visit www.dvgstar.com

GOOD LUCK

www.ingramcontent.com/pod-product-compliance
Lightning Source LLC
Chambersburg PA
CBHW071806170526
45167CB00003B/1188